My First Book about the Alphabet of Canidae (Wolves, Coyotes, Fox, & More)

Amazing Animal Books Children's Picture Books

By Molly Davidson

Mendon Cottage Books

JD-Biz Publishing

Read More Amazing Animal Books

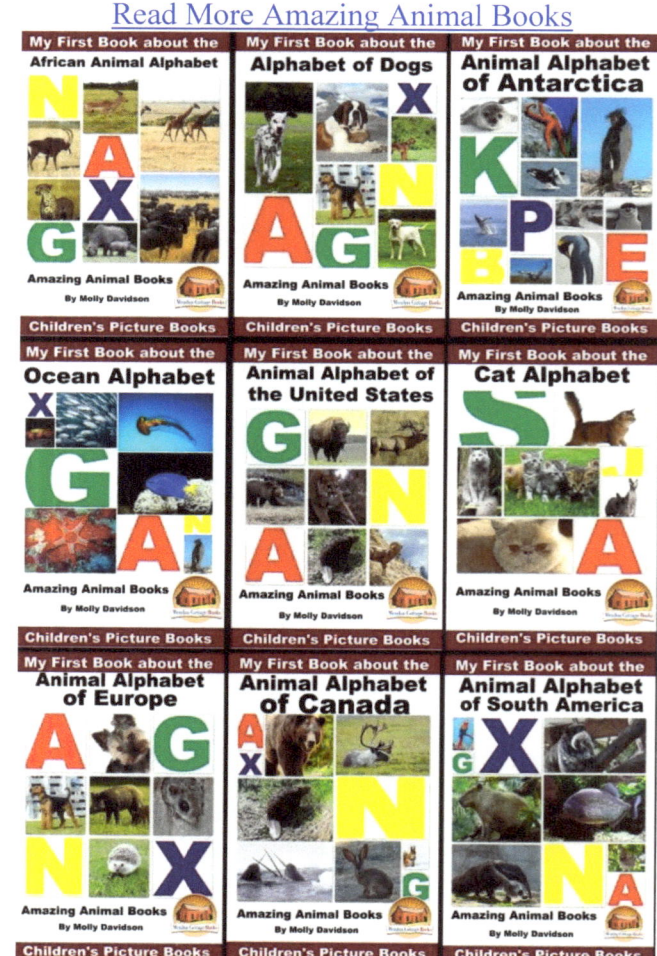

Purchase at Amazon.com

Download Free Books!
http://MendonCottageBooks.com

Introduction

Canidae are a species of four legged mammals that are carnivorous, which means meat eating.

The main species are wolves, jackals, foxes, coyotes, and dogs.

 **is for an Arctic Fox.**

Arctic foxes can survive in temperatures as cold as -58°F.

They have white fur in the winter to camouflage with the snow, and brown/gray fur in the summer to blend in with rocks.

 **is for a Bush Dog.**

Bush dogs live in families of up to 12 dogs in Central and South America.

They hunt as a group; some of the dogs chase the prey to water, usually paca, capybara, large birds, or monkeys, here the other dogs are waiting to attack.

B is also for a Black-Backed Jackal.

Black-backed jackals live in Africa, where they eat anything from bugs like beetles and grasshoppers to larger animals like sheep or impala.

They are found living in southeastern Africa.

C is for a Culpeo Fox.

Culpeo fox can be found on the western side of the Andes Mountains in South America.

They are the second largest canidae, behind the maned wolf, living in South America, boys can weighing up to 25 pounds.

C is also for a Crab-Eating Fox.

birdphotos.com © <u>Wikimedia Commons</u>

Crab-eating fox are a nocturnal, active at night, animal which lives in South America.

During the rainy season they eat crabs and other crustaceans, this is where they get their name from.

D is for a Dhole.

Dholes are found in Asia, living in packs of up to 40 dogs.

They make many different noises to communicate with each other; whistles, growls, screams, and clucks.

D is also for a Dingo.

Dingoes are an endangered species found in Australia and Southeast Asia.

They live in packs of about 10, and some mothers may kill pups that are not theirs in the pack!

 **is for an Ethiopian Wolf.**

An Ethiopian wolf is also called a Simien Wolf; it is the World's rarest canidae.

They live in Africa, mostly in the Bale Mountains, and are on the endangered list.

F is for a Fennec Fox.

The fennec fox is the smallest fox in the World, but it has the biggest ears, 6 inches long, compared to its body size.

G is for a Gray Wolf.

Gray wolves used to roam all over the Northern Hemisphere, but are now hardly seen in Europe and almost became extinct in the United States.

Gray wolves are the largest members of the canidae family, weighing up to 175 pounds.

 **is for a Hoary Fox.**

Elder Lagar © <u>Wikimedia Commons</u>

The hoary fox lives in Brazil where it is called raposinha - do - campo, in Portuguese, which means "meadow fox."

It is a small fox weighing less than 9 pounds.

I is for an Island Fox.

National Park Service, US Department of the Interior. © <u>Wikimedia Commons</u>

Island fox are a small fox only found on the Channel Islands of California.

They are a descended of the gray fox, but are much smaller and are more protected from predators, since they live on islands.

K  is for a Kit Fox.

Kit foxes are very common in the deserts of the western part of the United States.

Babies, called pups, live in the den for the first month then venture outside and they leave their mother around 6 months old.

L is for a Lycaon Pictus, the scientific name for an African Wild Dog.

African wild dogs live in groups, called packs, of up to 20, and are very caring toward other members of their group.

They hunt wildebeests and antelope as a pack.

M  is for a Maned Wolf.

Maned wolves are related to red and gray wolves found in North America, but they live in South America, and are more similar to a red fox.

They live in groups, called packs, of 6 - 10 wolves.

N is for a Nyctereutes Procyonoides, the scientific name for a Raccoon Dog.

Raccoon dogs have curved claws which help them climb trees and hold on to slippery prey.

Their fur is thick and brownish-gray in the winter, and then it turns reddish in the summer.

O

is for an Otocyon Megalotis, the scientific name for a Bat-Eared Fox.

Bat-eared fox leave on the African savannah and use their large ears to help keep them cool.

Their favorite food is termites found in acacia trees.

P is for a Pampas Fox.

Pampas fox live on lowlands, called pampas, in South America.

They usually live by themselves and are nocturnal, active at night.

 **R** is for a Red Fox.

Red fox can survive in most habitats; deserts, forests, mountains, grasslands, farms, and in peopled areas.

They use their thick tails as a warm cover in the cold and also as a warning signal of danger.

 **is for a Swift Fox.**

Swift foxes can run as fast as 30 miles per hour.

They are found in the grasslands of central North America.

They live 3 - 4 years in the wild.

S is also for a South American Gray Fox.

The South American gray fox is also called a Chilla, and are found living in the Andes Mountains.

T is for a Tibetan Sand Fox.

St. George Mivart © <u>Wikimedia Commons</u>

Tibetan sand fox have fur that give them a square face, and slit eyes.

U

is for an Urocyon Cinereoargenteus, the scientific name for a Gray Fox.

Gray fox are very common all over the United States and eat mostly rabbits, birds, and shrews.

They live in burrows of trees and stumps during the day, and hunt at night.

V

is for a Vulpes Vulpes, the scientific name for a Silver Fox.

Silver fox are the same as a red fox; they just have a different color of fur.

They have short under fur which helps keep them warm and longer outer fur for protection.

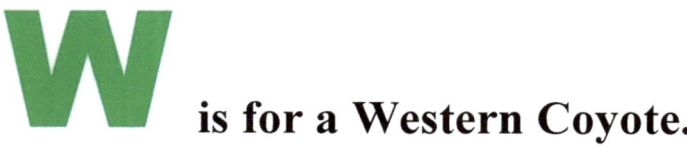 **is for a Western Coyote.**

Coyotes are great swimmers, and have been seen swimming in the ocean of distances up to 6 miles.

During the fall and winter they live in a pack which makes hunting easier.

Z is for a Zorro Culpeo.

Zorro Culpeos are also called an Andean Fox.

They will eat many things; some of their favorites are rabbits, rodents, and guanacos.

They are a pretty big canidae, some of the boys weigh up to 25 pounds.

Conclusion

I hope you have enjoyed reading this book about some of the amazing canidae animals.

One more fact, canidae are found all over the World, except Antarctica

Download Free Books!

http://MendonCottageBooks.com

Our books are available at

1. Amazon.com

2. Barnes and Noble

3. Itunes

4. Kobo

5. Smashwords

6. Google Play Books

Download Free Books!
http://MendonCottageBooks.com

Publisher

JD-Biz Corp

P O Box 374

Mendon, Utah 84325

http://www.jd-biz.com/

Mendon Cottage Books

P O Box 374, Mendon Utah 84325

www.ingramcontent.com/pod-product-compliance
Lightning Source LLC
Chambersburg PA
CBHW040746010626
45792CB00027B/667